The American Colonies

The
Georgia Colony

by Tyler Schumacher

Capstone
press

Mankato, Minnesota

Fact Finders is published by Capstone Press,
151 Good Counsel Drive, P.O. Box 669, Mankato, Minnesota 56002.
www.capstonepress.com

Library of Congress Cataloging-in-Publication Data
Schumacher, Tyler.
    The Georgia colony / by Tyler Schumacher.
    p. cm.—(Fact Finders. The American colonies)
    Includes bibliographical references and index.
    ISBN 0-7368-2674-2 (hardcover)
    1. Georgia—History—Colonial period, ca. 1600–1775—Juvenile literature. I. Title. II.
American colonies (Capstone Press)
F289.S27 2006
975.8'02—dc22   2005000125

Summary: An introduction to the history, government, economy, resources, and people of
    the Georgia Colony. Includes maps and charts.

Editorial Credits
Katy Kudela, editor; Jennifer Bergstrom, set designer, illustrator, and book designer;
    Bobbi J. Dey, book designer; Wanda Winch, photo researcher/photo editor

Photo Credits
Cover image: View of Savannah, Georgia, The Granger Collection, New York

The Bridgeman Art Library/The Stapleton Collection, 16–17
Corbis/Bettmann, 23
Ed Jackson, 11, 29 (left)
The Granger Collection, New York, 6, 7, 12–13, 14, 21
North Wind Picture Archives, 4–5, 15, 19, 26–27, 29 (right)
Stock Montage Inc., 10

**Capstone Press wishes to thank Glenn T. Eskew, Associate Professor of History,
Georgia State University, Atlanta, Georgia, for his assistance with this project.**

1 2 3 4 5 6 10 09 08 07 06 05

Table of Contents

~ Chapter 1 ~
Georgia's First People

Thousands of years ago, American Indians settled the land now known as Georgia. These people became known as the Creek and Cherokee. The Creek lived in the southern flatlands. The Cherokee settled in the Appalachian Mountains to the north.

Daily Life

The Cherokee and Creek grew corn, beans, and squash. They also hunted bears, deer, and birds. Along the coast, the Creek gathered oysters and clams. They fished the rivers for bass and trout.

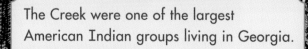

The Creek were one of the largest American Indian groups living in Georgia.

The Creek lived in villages of about 1,000 people. They built huts with roofs of wood or bark. Each village had a plaza in its center. Dances, games, and ceremonies took place in the plaza.

Cherokee villages were much like those of the Creek. The Cherokee built their homes out of wood, grass, and mud. Each village had a large hall for meetings and special events.

Catholic missionaries came to North America to spread their religion.

European Arrival

During the 1540s, Spanish explorers sailed to Creek and Cherokee lands. They searched for gold but found none.

The British and the French also explored the land. They wanted to trade with the American Indians for deer hides to sell in Europe.

In the late 1500s, Spanish **missionaries** came to North America. They tried to spread the Catholic religion to the Indians.

American Indians traded animal skins and furs for European goods. ➡

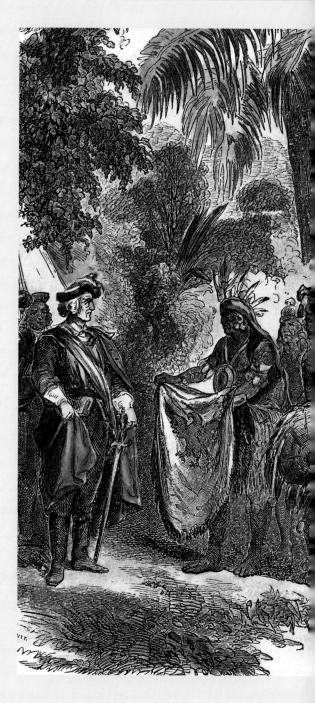

~ Chapter 2 ~

Early Settlers

In the early 1700s, poor people in Great Britain had few opportunities. Those who could not pay their bills were sent to jail. Britain's prisons were crowded. The British government wanted a solution. The parliament asked its member, James Edward Oglethorpe, to offer solutions. Oglethorpe suggested an American colony. He thought the colony could be settled by people who had fallen on hard times.

Great Britain had 12 colonies in North America. Spain had settled the area to their south. Spain and Britain fought for control of the land between them. The British hoped a new southern colony would keep Spain out of the wealthy Carolina area.

Georgia was called debatable land. Both Great Britain and Spain wanted to control the land. By 1763, Georgia's borders were set. ➡

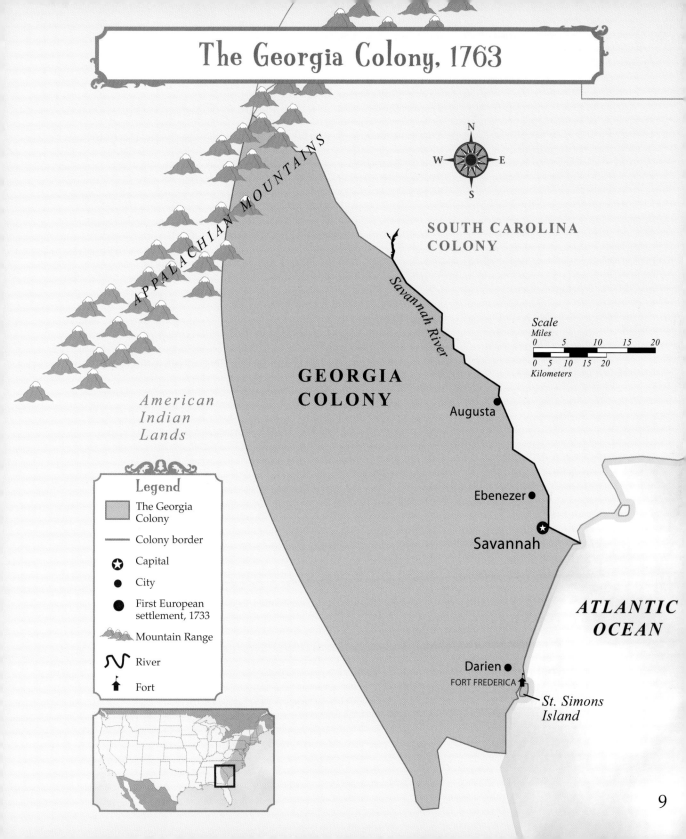

The Georgia Colony, 1763

APPALACHIAN MOUNTAINS

SOUTH CAROLINA
COLONY

Savannah River

American
Indian
Lands

GEORGIA
COLONY

Augusta

Scale
Miles
0   5   10   15   20
0   10   15   20
Kilometers

Ebenezer

Savannah

ATLANTIC
OCEAN

Legend

The Georgia
Colony

Colony border

Capital

City

First European
settlement, 1733

Mountain Range

River

Fort

Darien

FORT FREDERICA

St. Simons
Island

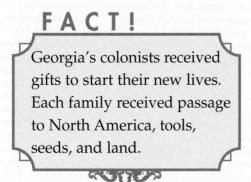

James Oglethorpe brought people over from Great Britain to settle the Georgia Colony.

In 1732, King George II of England gave a land **charter** to a group of men called trustees. The trustees named the colony Georgia in honor of the king.

Many people wanted to join the new colony. The trustees picked people with special skills. They chose carpenters, sawyers, and other craftsmen to build the new colony.

Settlers Arrive

In 1733, the trustees sent a group of 120 English settlers to start the colony in Georgia. James Oglethorpe served as the colony's leader.

F A C T !

Georgia's colonists received gifts to start their new lives. Each family received passage to North America, tools, seeds, and land.

Oglethorpe picked a bluff above the Savannah River for the colony's first settlement. The settlers named the city Savannah.

Treaty with the Creek

The English settlers soon wanted more land. Oglethorpe became friends with the Creek Indians who lived nearby. One of the Creek leaders, Tomochichi, helped Oglethorpe organize a treaty with 50 other Creek chiefs. This agreement allowed the British to settle on land the Creek did not use.

▲ Tomochichi helped Oglethorpe create a land treaty with a group of 50 Creek chiefs.

Chapter 3

Colonial Life

The colonists found Georgia a difficult place to live. Settlers had to clear forests to build towns and plant crops. They sometimes fought with the Indians and other European colonists.

Many settlers died of yellow fever during their first summer in Savannah. William Cox, Georgia's first doctor, died after only three months. A boat of Jewish settlers arrived that same year with a doctor on board.

War with Spain

In 1739, a war broke out between Great Britain and Spain. Battles took place in southern Georgia and Florida.

Savannah was Georgia's first settlement. It also served as the colony's capital.

The Spanish attacked Georgia in 1742. The Battle of Bloody Marsh took place near Fort Frederica on St. Simons Island. Oglethorpe and his troops won the battle. They secured Georgia's land for Great Britain.

James Oglethorpe thought the sickness in Savannah might be caused by drinking alcohol. In 1733, he stopped rum trading in the colony.

Early settlers learned many new skills, from dyeing their clothing to growing their own crops. ▼

Loyalty to Britain

In their new home, Georgians stayed loyal to Great Britain. They celebrated King George II's birthday. On the king's birthday, colonists raised the British flag and fired their guns.

Food in the Colony

At first, the colonists couldn't grow enough to eat. They bought rice, wheat, and flour from settlers in South Carolina. Later, colonists planted peas, corn, squash, and rice to feed themselves.

Georgians ate many other types of food. They hunted deer, turkeys, and geese. They fished in the Savannah River.

During colonial times, there were few public schools. By the 1800s, America's school system had grown.

Education

Schools in Georgia were similar to those in the other southern colonies. Large cities had schools. In Savannah, children could learn reading, writing, math, and religion. Areas far from the cities often did not have schools. Preachers taught lessons in church.

Chapter 4

Work and Trade

Georgia's first colonists tried to grow olives and grapes. They also tried to make silk. These projects failed. Georgia's climate was not right for growing olives and grapes, or for raising silkworms.

Colonists soon found crops that grew well in Georgia. The wet coastal area was good for planting rice and **indigo**. Wheat, corn, and peas grew well farther inland.

Forest products and livestock were also important. Georgia's large forests provided lumber. Trees produced tar. Settlers also raised cattle, pigs, and horses.

Plantations were large farms in the Georgia Colony. Indigo was one of the crops grown.

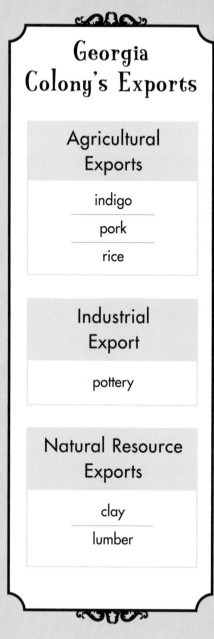

Georgia Colony's Exports

Agricultural Exports
indigo
pork
rice

Industrial Export
pottery

Natural Resource Exports
clay
lumber

Most Georgians worked on small farms. A few farmers owned large **plantations**. Plantation owners needed many workers. The trustees had made it illegal to own slaves. Instead, colonists used **indentured servants**.

In 1749, the trustees changed their law. They decided to allow slaves in Georgia. Colonists bought slaves to work in their fields.

Not every colonist was a farmer. Bakers, shoemakers, and bricklayers worked in Georgia. Woodcutters and carpenters also set up shops.

Trade

People in Georgia could not make everything they needed. Colonists traded with Britain and the West Indies. They also traded with American Indians. Often, Indians would trade furs to the colonists and receive guns in return.

F A C T !

Augusta became an important trading town in Georgia. It sat at the crossroads of several American Indian trails.

Georgia colonists could go to stores to buy clothing from Great Britain. ➤

Chapter 5

Community and Faith

In Europe, people were sometimes punished because of their religious beliefs. Those people often came to the American colonies. Some of them came to Georgia.

Different Religions

As leader of the colony, James Oglethorpe allowed religious freedom for many colonists. Lutherans fleeing from Germany arrived in the early 1730s. They left their home country because they wanted to be able to practice their religion.

The Highland Scots were another group to settle in the American colonies. Some came to Georgia. They brought their Presbyterian religion with them.

James Oglethorpe welcomed
the Highland Scots to Georgia.

23

Catholics were the only religious group not allowed in Georgia. The colony's government did not approve of Catholics because of Britain's war with France and Spain. Both countries supported the Catholic religion. Great Britain followed the Church of England.

Population Growth of the Georgia Colony

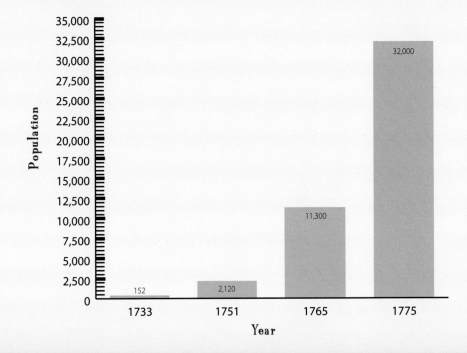

Official Religion

In 1758, Georgia's government made the Church of England its official religion. The government divided the colony into 12 **parishes**. Each parish built its own English church. These churches kept records of births, marriages, and deaths.

Colonists had to pay a church tax. This money supported priests and the poor. People were not forced to join the Church of England. But all groups had to pay the church tax.

▲ Georgian settlers often carried guns to protect themselves on their walks to church.

FACT!

One Georgia law said all people had to bring their guns to church in case of an attack. Georgians feared attacks from American Indians and the Spanish.

Chapter 6

Becoming a State

In 1752, the trustees gave up their charter to the British king. The king chose a governor to rule Georgia. The colonists also elected assembly members. At first, Georgians were happy to follow Britain's rules. Over time, their happiness faded.

Growing Apart

During the mid-1700s, Britain fought a costly war with Spain and France. The French and Indian War (1754–1763) left Britain deeply in debt.

To raise money, the British parliament heavily taxed the colonies. The colonists became angry. Some people spoke of forming their own government.

Georgia was the last of the 13 colonies to form. It was part of an area called the Southern Colonies. ➡

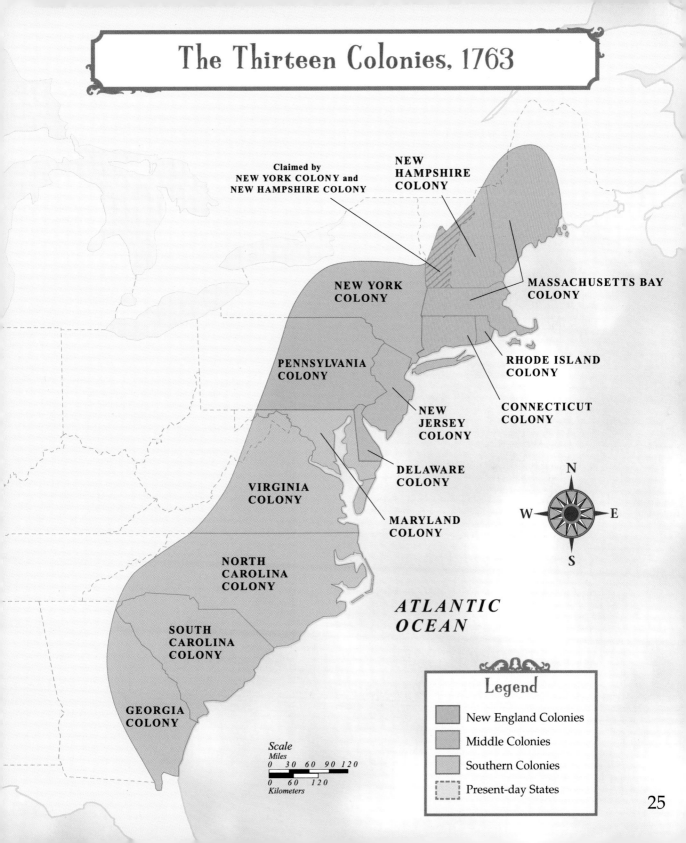

The Thirteen Colonies, 1763

Claimed by
NEW YORK COLONY and
NEW HAMPSHIRE COLONY

NEW
HAMPSHIRE
COLONY

NEW YORK
COLONY

MASSACHUSETTS BAY
COLONY

PENNSYLVANIA
COLONY

RHODE ISLAND
COLONY

NEW
JERSEY
COLONY

CONNECTICUT
COLONY

DELAWARE
COLONY

VIRGINIA
COLONY

MARYLAND
COLONY

NORTH
CAROLINA
COLONY

*ATLANTIC
OCEAN*

SOUTH
CAROLINA
COLONY

N

W   E

S

GEORGIA
COLONY

Scale
Miles
0   30   60   90   120

0   60   120
Kilometers

Legend

New England Colonies

Middle Colonies

Southern Colonies

Present-day States

A New Government

Colonial leaders held a meeting in 1774 to talk about the problems with Britain. Georgia did not send anyone to this First Continental Congress. But the colony agreed to support plans made at the meeting.

In 1775, all 13 colonies sent members to the Second Continental Congress. The following year, Congress signed the Declaration of Independence. The document said that the colonies no longer belonged to Britain. The American colonies called themselves the United States.

Colonists Go to War

Britain did not agree with the declaration. The colonies fought for their independence in the Revolutionary War (1775–1783). During the war, British soldiers captured Savannah and Augusta. British soldiers occupied these cities for most of the war. After several battles, Americans pushed the British out of Savannah. America won the war in 1783.

In 1787, American leaders wrote a new plan to govern the nation. On January 2, 1788, Georgia approved the U.S. **Constitution**. It became the fourth state to join the United States.

◀ During the Revolutionary War, the British captured the city of Savannah.

Fast Facts

Name
The Georgia Colony
(named for King George II
of England)

Location
Southern colonies

Year of Founding
1733

First Settlement
Savannah

Colony's Founder
James Oglethorpe

Religious Faiths
Church of England, French
Huguenot, Jewish, Lutheran,
Moravian, Presbyterian

Agricultural Products
Corn, indigo, peas, rice, wheat

Major Industries
Logging, trade

Population in 1775
32,000 people

Statehood
January 2, 1788
(4th state)

Time Line

1749
Slavery is made legal in Georgia.

1763
Proclamation of 1763 sets colonial borders and provides land for American Indians.

1776
Declaration of Independence is approved in July.

1733
The first treaty with Creek Indians is signed, giving settlers land.

1758
The Church of England becomes the official religion of Georgia.

1783
America wins the Revolutionary War.

1775
American colonies begin fight for their independence from Great Britain in the Revolutionary War.

1732
King George II allows trustees to start the colony of Georgia.

1788
On January 2, Georgia is the fourth state to join the United States.

1754-1763
British and French soldiers fight the French and Indian War in North America.

Glossary

charter (CHAR-tur)—an official document that grants permission to create a city or colony and provides for a government

constitution (kon-stuh-TOO-shuhn)—the written system of laws in a state or country that state the rights of the people and the powers of the government

indentured servant (in-DEN-churd SUR-vuhnt)—someone who agrees to work for another person for a certain length of time in exchange for travel expenses, food, or housing

indigo (IN-duh-goh)—a crop grown on plantations for trade purposes; colonists used indigo to make blue dye.

missionary (MISH-uh-nair-ee)—someone who is sent by a church or religious group to teach that group's faith and do good works, especially in a foreign country

parish (PA-rish)—an area or group of people that has its own church minister or priest

plantation (plan-TAY-shuhn)—a large farm where crops such as coffee, tea, tobacco, and cotton are grown

Internet Sites

FactHound offers a safe, fun way to find Internet sites related to this book. All of the sites on FactHound have been researched by our staff.

Here's how:

1. Visit *www.facthound.com*
2. Type in this special code **0736826742** for age-appropriate sites. Or enter a search word related to this book for a more general search.
3. Click on the **Fetch It** button.

FactHound will fetch the best sites for you!

Read More

Davis, Marc. *The Georgia Colony.* Our Thirteen Colonies. Chanhassen, Minn.: Child's World, 2003.

Lassieur, Allison. *The Creek Nation.* Native Peoples. Mankato, Minn.: Capstone Press, 2002.

Walsh, Kieran. *James Oglethorpe.* Discover the Life of a Colonial American. Vero Beach, Fla.: Rourke, 2005.

Index